Jongleur in the Courtyard

Mandy Pannett

Mandy X

Indigo Dreams Publishing

First Edition: Jongleur in the Courtyard
First published in Great Britain in 2015 by:
Indigo Dreams Publishing
24 Forest Houses
Halwill
Beaworthy
EX21 5UU

www.indigodreams.co.uk

Mandy Pannett has asserted her right under the Copyright,
Designs and Patents Act 1988 to be identified as the author of
this work.
©2015 Mandy Pannett

ISBN 978-1-909357-81-5

British Library Cataloguing in Publication Data. A CIP record
for this book can be obtained from the British Library.

Designed and typeset in Palatino Linotype by Indigo Dreams.
Cover design by Ronnie Goodyer at Indigo Dreams

Printed and bound in Great Britain by 4edge Ltd.
www.4edge.co.uk

Papers used by Indigo Dreams are recyclable products made
from wood grown in sustainable forests following the guidance
of the Forest Stewardship Council.

For Maureen Caliendo

Acknowledgements:

Versions of the poems have appeared in Tears in the Fence, The North, Envoi, Agenda, Hemeneutics Chaos Journal, Ecotopia Strangeness (Squircle Line Press), 'In Protest' (Human Rights Consortium poetry anthology), 'Remembrance' (Rhyme and Reason anthology), 'Sharp as Lemons' (Earlyworks Press prize winning flash and poetry anthology), 'The Genesis of Falcon' (Sentinel Poetry Movement).

'You Say You Don't Do Smiles' was a runner up the Cardiff International Poetry Competition 2014.
'Ptolemy's Stars' won 1st prize in the Barnet Poetry Competition 2014.
'Lantern Girl' won 2nd prize in the Segora Poetry Competition 2014
'If Touched by Fingernails of Sun' won 2nd prize in The Red Shed Competition 2013.
'Scatterings from Hogarth' was Highly Commended in the Mere Poetry Festival 2013
'Fine Detail' was a runner up in the Perform Poetry Competition 2012 and 'Pseudonymous' in 2013.
'A Marrying of Herbs' was commended in the Sentinel Annual Poetry Competition' 2013.

As always, my love and thanks for their support to family and friends. Special thanks to Caroline Maldonado who has patiently read countless drafts and edits of the poems and shown the same care and apparent interest with each version.

Previous Publications by Mandy Pannett:

Bee Purple, Oversteps Books, 2002
Frost Hollow, Oversteps Books, 2006
Allotments in the Orbital, Searle Publishing, 2009
All the Invisibles, SPM Publications, 2012
The Onion Stone (Novella), Pewter Rose Press, 2011

CONTENTS

Jongleur in the Courtyard

SMALL PART
Ancient Egyptians believed the soul was composed of five parts:

Heart

Easy to have
an out-of-balance heart
when a feather tip of love or distrust
makes all the difference.

Shadow

Between light in the air
and the light on stone
an umbra darkens

and the starling's silhouette is contoured
like a drone's.

Name

At school he covered
his hatreds, mostly, that misfit boy.
Every day he hid
the register of pupils, every day
it turned up in a bin.
If their names were lost, he later said
I hoped they'd vanish too.

Essence

Where some see ugliness
in slime mould, call it dog's vomit, detest
the way it feasts on rot and creeps
through trees in yellow-
wet threads, others
see beauty

in these cells, these singular
messes of life.

Spirit

... and we might raise
our arms to the sky, tease out
light and scatters of blue as loop by
loop we crochet a shawl, a mantle
to shelter our breath –

if only we could, if only
we knew how.

UNSAVEABLE

The moth in me twitches
in frail light like a rapid
flash dancer or text on a screen

saved like nostalgia
on a quick memory stick where yearning
may quiver again into life –

A prayer may sing from a minaret
but I am unfriended by

gods of my youth
who doze now with angels or shift
a few posts

but won't hear an update
in ninety quick-firing
seconds of news

or a one minute clip
about wheat and good corn
wasted by lords of the sun

SOME WOODWORM

crawl from chests of drawers
like roman cohorts stiff with dust

dazzled
by the sudden light
and cursed in their fleeing
for the spoil they leave

but mostly
they die in tunnels

poor miserable atoms
choked with the fruits
of their soft plunderings

and wiped out
in all the darkness
that once
was chosen as home

TALKING TO WILLIAM BLAKE ABOUT HIS 'GHOST OF A FLEA'

Once you saw angels
in delicate trees, heaven in a wild flower.
Out of what nightmarish pit of hell does this ghost
come following you?

What heartburn, what acid in your gut
vomits this bile?

This is not an intricate flea.
It is muscular, pugnacious, flat-footed
and stamping on stars.

A spirit should be pale and thin, glide in the mist ...

This is no ghost.
Ghosts don't dribble, drop sulphur farts, stink of garlic and egg.

Let me
get rid of it for you.

I will itch the creature
into the fur of the urban fox who tips
bins over and scoffs chicken gristle, thai rice, seepings
of gorgonzola cheese.

Shall we sit down and watch the fox
scratch and scratch and scratch at his ear
until that flea, shredded by claws,
disintegrates in air?

This was something evil and small:
a dissonance
the other side of vision.

Dreamer
it's morning; a new day.

Let your eyelashes
flicker, lift
open to the light.

LANTERN GIRL

In the hullabaloo of his return
the backpack of the prodigal son
was shoved in a cupboard beneath the stairs

dark on the straps with sweat of the road
tied up at the neck like the Thanksgiving turkey
they'd fattened and eaten for days.

Five months later he drags the bag
out into the light, unzips a pocket, discovers
one half of a one-way ticket, the tattered

remains of the Dear John letter
that last girl sent, two empty cartons
of blueberry juice and a twist

of white tissue with seeds
from a pumpkin, bits of old flesh
clinging on.

Yes, he remembers
that pumpkin: a harvest sale
of autumn fruits, discarded gourds

too pitted to sell, a girl
who had gone to the sun of a pumpkin
and carved them a lantern for night.

Well now he's returned
to the wedge of demands; goodbye
long-travellin' road ...

He'll settle for life
with a needy old man and maybe
forget that very last girl

who gave him a pumpkin
with light in its eyes and left him
the seeds in a bag.

LACE, FAR OFF

A tangle of berries and orange rowan –
as foragers we try to snaffle
the sweet-sour fruit
before an attentive bird.

This is a time for folklore tales,
a day for dalliance in the woods,
lovers reach up to branches of hazel
and go a-nutting for joy.

... how easily the elderberries
slip through my fingers into a dish;
their empty stems are spaces of airiness,
delicate-bare as lace.

Once this day was special for women
who were given a candle at twilight
and a scrape of gin to bathe their eyes
so they could make their lace with comfort
for more hours.

Such hedgerow goodness in my house
as apples bubble in pans ...

By evening the stems are compost.
In murky light they have the look
of fingers, flattened

and thin as the fingers of those
who sew cheap clothes through endless
sessions
for outlets far away.

Today I found no hazel trees
but chestnuts are swelling
inside their shells

with prickles tiny and soft as stitches
and the discomfort, the pain
of touching them
still a long way off.

SCATTERINGS FROM HOGARTH

This woman is winter, not an Aurora
goddess of dawn.
Single-minded in the market, she ignores
all paupers who shiver in snow, for she is not cold;
only in her inner self is she like ice.

Footprints from her furry boots mark her steps.
A red-nosed and sneezing boy follows close behind.
No Wenceslas against the winter's rage
she is on her way to church and has no time.

No backcloth here of snow-capped hills.
Only slabs of white dirt on the roofs.

It is springtime in Soho at noon;
each man stuffed inside his world.

No one observes a hungry child
who scrapes a doorway for scatters of food.
Someone kicks a cat, rotting, into the gutter.

There is not a speck of joy
in this dour street.

It may be an Islington summer's evening
but heat is claustrophobic.

A mother, oblivious to her brood,
is sweaty and heavy, close to her time –
as is the dog who, parched with thirst,
looks longingly at the river,
the shelter of green vine.

The dark side of autumn:
Hades is one night at Charing Cross.
Homeless people shiver, crouch in nooks.
Onlookers have faces of pigs.

A fire from somebody's vehicle
lights the city's sky.

This is autumn at its end:
wretched and stripped.

THE OTHER SIDE OF APPEARANCES

this leaf
this small cupped leaf
whispers a soliloquy

about its heart
which is a pitcher trap for insects
dissolving in green cells

dark as a vivid triptych
when both its wings are shut
dark as prisons

where forgotten men
bright as robins or a red-fur fox
turn into pelts

IF TOUCHED BY FINGERNAILS

of sun
a troll in folklore turns to rock.
Whether the process is haemorrhage swift
or slower in pain as small bones set
who knows –

Certainly not that victim
of heaven's barbaric revenge:
Lot's wife, carcass in salt
mashed by a liquid blitz of light
to a whitened root.

Of course she looked behind her
half-turning to check they were safe –
she'd have raced back to those melting cities
and dragged her daughters out
of that brimstone's heart.

A MARRYING OF HERBS

I'm making a soup, adding in carrots
with coriander, parsley and stock, musing
on the sound of *dissolve* which is an elusive
long-limbed word, languid
as hush – but is also

a word for dispersal – a scatter of seeds
on too thin a soil, a small pulled thread on a cardigan's
hem which begins its tedious unravelling.

Better to see it as an overlap, a gradual
transition from one image to the next
where the change in perspective is apparent
only when the film ends.

There are measures of harshness here:
a dismal resolution as in a shrine
reformed, made friable, disburdened
of all its monastery stone –

No. Stone is too hard a word.
Dissolution should shine like a crystal
of beryl, be sea-water blue, liquid
as aquamarine ...

O *dissolvere, dissolvere,*
are you a ripple from a gondolier's oar
or a subtle loosening of life –
earth in Juliet's breath?

WHIFF OF MOUSE

An aged museum with a whiff of mouse
sunrise through pale-green windows too dusty
to see through or show that it's not a new season
still less than spring, no more than a piecemeal
diminishment of winter. Bones in cardboard boxes
nestle in bits: labels hint at teeth, tusks, splinters
of wishbone, a sea-eagle's vertebrae, claws
from one small wader. On a shelf is an algal
bloom of minerals and rock from a fallen star.
These are not orchids in a hot-house –
lacerated by winds they were sundered apart
from a precious rooting. Here is the debris
of ransacked cities, rubble with traceries
fine as the backbones of sprats.

SPOON AND SWORD WITH A COFFIN LID

1
Little spoon
you fill the spaces of my thoughts with reindeer
tiny and spiky as thorns on a hill

and my imagination
heaves both you and myself awake
at this carving of horn and the hand that whittled
a perfect stag
onto the scoop of your bowl.

2
You would have been
a rich man's weapon, blade in a river
surfacing like Excalibur
(or a bit of it)
during a ring-road dig.

What offering were you
to a Roman god
what appeasement or great wish?

3
Gilded now in museum light
you are preserved –
or the one remaining
side of you is, for you were the first
of six strong sides
around a coffin of lead.

Where is your vault and broken stone?
Dispersed in earth and air
like a chantry mass no longer sung
for a soul's relief

though wealth was paid and set aside
for indefinite
centuries of prayer.

MAMMOTH, PART OF ME

Mammoth, part of me
would see you revamped as clone.
I could stroke your fuzz, so
orange-blond soft, feel the hard
and swelling buds
where your marvellous tusks will grow

But this is selfishness, my wanting;
this is greed.
Mammoth, you must not quicken again
in a cold unwelcoming world.

With those tusks
you would become the poachers' prey
for they are priceless and, to some,
worth murdering for.

I will forego the joy
of seeing you feast on a blackthorn hedge
crunching it up, twig and splinter,
like marrow, like bone DNA.

CHARIOTEER

He grips the reins
with his only hand; tendon-like
they stretch, outstretch.
His lost arm's
a muscle-gone spasm
of clench.

Of horses, some bits:
one damaged ear, shoe of a hoof.
Apollo has snatched the chariot
into his dust.

Slave, you will wait a very long time
at the starting post.
Your eyes
sad, sharp, glass.

DEATH: AN EXHIBITION

In this Museum of Death
a series of nudes cavorts on blossom
and slow, voluptuous grass

Later they are morphing
into skulls

Who escapes?

Outside this window
someone once strolled in a stubble field
musing on starlings, strips of long river, the fruitfulness
of mid-December dusk

while another man heard
the strike of a clock, and though the snow
was high on the road (higher than his horse's belly)
he set out to make love
to somebody somewhere –

Listen: there's a violin
bowed by a long thigh bone

Quis evadet?

MY ENGLISH BLOSSOM TREE

is April in snow, now heavy
now lingering

as Hiroshige's
soft white feather-flakes touch
a mandarin duck

on its green river
under the cover of tall
thin reeds as even

more drops tumble down
on sparrows, camellias
bamboo on a hill ...

a moment of pause
for snow that is longed for
in seasons of drought

'THREE FRIENDS AND A HUNDRED BIRDS'
(Painting by Bian Wenjin, circa 1356-1428)

How noisy it must be –
not only assorted passerine calls
but a cacophony of feathers
like those of the scarlet minaret who flies away
with a beak of bugs flushed from the bark
by his adamant throbbing of wings.

Such a lot of birds –
surely no tree this side of paradise
has so many – and someone has counted them,
listed and numbered by name and position –
but there are only ninety-seven –
where are the rest?

Are they Eurasian Sparrows
lower on the trunk but fluffed up in embarrassment,
self-effacing and out of sight?

Or perhaps the artist was weary
his fingers tired of plumage and leaves.
Or maybe he lost count.

They are beautiful birds, perfect
in detail: even the Orange-Bellied Leaf Bird
is golden on its leaf.

And such names: Siberian Robin, Oriental
Skylark, a Slatey-Blue Flycatcher perches up high
with three Laughing Thrushes, each one
with a different throat.

Three friends are here as blessings
in this busy winter scene:

pine, bamboo and blossom of plum –
blossom which flourishes best in snow
and whose fragrance is strong in a gale.

AGREE A SEPARATION

and we could watch the city sparrows
pecking around this station bar
blown in by the windy platform's
draught from a leaving train

and we'd discuss why Russian starlings
seek out the cold of our southern shores
or recall a night in the Welney Fens
where rivers were silver under the moon
and the wetlands wild with geese

we might remember the seagull again
who mistook our bedroom window for sky
and how the smear of its small face
stayed on the glass for hours

and we'd agree a separation
would be painful too
and wonder if the bird survived
to lift its wings and fly again though
bruised – we hope it tried, we'd say
we hope it really tried

RAVEN, MY DOOM

sitter in high trees
why have you condemned my love
to moulder in a warrior's grave?

Corbie bird, your call was soft
in our highland years.
No piper's lament, no omen.

I am weary of dreams
that offer reflection of my own self
but do not yield him back

though imagination
in these hours of sleep
may reel and spin in exquisite belief

that we might say
what we always intended to say
but never did.

YOU SAY YOU DON'T DO SMILES

don't like drawing them,
never learnt the technique.

You're lying.

If it was that simple you would paint
only angels, colourless as moons and dripping
with lilies
like couriers for flowers online.

If it was that simple
you'd give me a low-lipped, dour expression
and let me turn around.

Instead you paint
my back, always my back
so that the moody outline of me
mingles with the umbrage of an artificial beach
or an apartment block where even verandas
are in profile, but I am not.

Will you buy me a drink tonight
share some supper for once?
I'll get us the table nearest the door
you know I will.

Better still, paint me a towel.
Lay it down on that balcony, third from the left.
I'll strip my clothes off, find a bikini, be a small
red dot to focus the eye, a reference point for scale ...

Not your style?

You say you like your canvases
minimalist and bleak –
silence
in a bloody, anguished world.

So if love in the sand dunes isn't for us
then I may as well be faceless
sparse as spinifex grass

and since there's nothing
to be happy about
I'm glad you never do smiles.

IN SHORT, NORDIC
(The tale of Skadi and Njord, two gods)

1.

   Narrator:

It begins on the windward side of winter, a cold blue place where a gentle slipper of events has never been kicked by an iron-clad boot – until the day an ogre, more monstrous than a dozen leviathans, gives birth in his armpits to a tribe of gods who mutilate his muscle, testicle, eyebrow, bone and skin – all of which items shape into Midgard, a human world where even shadows are flayed.

   Skadi:

There's something about
his outstretched foot, the shape
of his buttocks, his long legs
that captures me ...
and his eyes – I like the deep-
sea blue of them, the way his lips
taste of salt, the way his hair
is tousled
like seal fur blowing back.

2.

   Narrator:

At the start it is spring – bright sky, buds of hope. There is melody too, a meandering line but in unison with harmony. Always there's the drone, the single long note like a psaltery played below the voice, the vibration, the hum: 'We Are One, We Are One, We Are One.'

He will be her troubadour, bringing her songs of the people, songs of the sea, a foot-tapping pulse, the lightness of 'In Dulce Jubilo'. She is

drawn to the minor key, happiest with Wagner and a pair of riding
boots. 'Misere Mei Deus' threads her dreams.

3.

Njord:

This is becoming a white marriage.
Strange how two
can equal zero, how proximity
may come to mean
a long way out of reach.

Sea-winds flying in at dawn
over the rocking sea, the bucking wave,
fan into life the flames of this
our funeral pyre.

Skadi:

Sometimes, almost
I can hear them –
even in this salty sea-dump, this
flat and forsaken patch of pebbles
that you call home –
some reindeer, hesitant
beyond my fence, those snow-
shovelling diggers of sedge,
knee bones click-clicking,
prick-ears poised
for the keening of wolf.

I am sick of the sea-mews cry
and starlings that blacken light.

I ache for the whine of a mountain dog.

4.

Njord:

There are many gods
and man must find his own.
We, creeping merrily out of a saga
thought we could shrug

complications off,
hear the coda of the whale,
its underhum of love.

How easy it seemed:
one month in your mountains, Skadi,
one by my blue sea.

You would grow accustomed to gulls,
the harbour's hubub
and all the fishing talk.

My nerves, like iron-clad bells
would soon learn
the cadences of skiing,

the silences of your ice.

5.

Narrator:

*Yes, it seemed possible. Sunrise would be golden – a taste of butter
after the dark; winter, on a tender shore, would always be warm.*

*Yet they were wrong. Their lovers' whispers are now dispersing,
slight as breezes, in acres of different fields.*

A LAUDANUM TINT

and still he keeps on painting
though many critics rubbish his work
say it's dreary and dead as pork, deride
his skies whose sunsets are grim
in their heavy laudanum tints.
Here are folk in a moody gloom
(as if they've never heard of a smile)
for his is a canvas patterned in *noir* –
stark, gothic, obscure and bleak with
silhouettes like flies on glass or shadows
who are leaving. Still he keeps on painting
until he's content with his low-lit dreams
the melt of frost on winter grass
a warmth of pigments touching

PSEUDONYMOUS

Cynewulf, the arc of the sun
swings more fiercely over this world
since you were here

We are reduced
to an ache of the heart
and the thinnest of thin gold leaf –

Thin gold leaf – unlike
the rood, that shimmer in gold of your vision-tree –
oh the bliss, you cried, the bliss
of such a dream

which now shimmers
into distance
as even the best dreams do

and whatever that bloody tree learned in its life
creeps off
to a brown-rot mould

And of you, voice-bearer, what fibre is left?
Your name's an acrostic in a script
a tentative runic signature
nestled in text

Why this scarcely observable
gesture, this cryptic indication
you too were here?

Dream on, poor fellow –
we shall all be anonymous soon

IN ICE AND IRON

Snatching at flies in the air seems, for us, foot-
rooted us, an instinctive thing, as if vision might brighten at the
squashing, the loss of some dirty kiss.

Pointless, for the sky is no clearer now
than it was on the day we once looked up, ancient foragers in
ice and iron, desperate

for the sudden halt, silence of wings, the calculated
drop of birds whose ferocious scavenging led us racing to the
spot, the grabbing of raw, red meat.

Now we've forgotten how to look at the sky, let alone look
through it or go beyond the faces of stars
fresh dead when man hit flint.

Can you hear the wind, hear absence of wind, creakings in the
permafrost, the crawling of segmented bits and pieces on the
sea bed left over from the Great

Dying, that mass eradication of insects by a large impactor? Yet,
even as a trickster shifts
from salamander into heat, his name (sparrow-

soft in a tabby's mouth) is caught. So we offer
identity to a meteorite, or rock of it, call it *Woman, Wigwam, Dog*
–words to cling to and pin down –

words from the bedrock of soil. A solution then, somewhere in
the interludes, those dark interludes where our ancestors lived
in the time

before fire – or when having found how to kindle
a flame they lost the secret and rested awhile
with little vision and always the smell of dust.

THIS ONE WORD
(The story referred to is Franz Kafka's 'The Bucket Rider')

Winter. Worse than winter.
Kafka shivers, coughs in Berlin
begins a fragment short as breath
about a man who has no coal, hypothermic
and half alive. Phrases halt
at semi-colons, words are cold as rime.

Change of action, change of scene.
Peering into his cellar of thought
the author finds a bucket that flies ...

and we fly too with hope for the man
for treasure itself may be disguised
in a plastic bag or cardboard box and still
be a magical gift.

So now we have a bucket
that our hero sits upon: a bucket like
a camel squatting, rising to a stately height
and a dozen lines of dialogue
a buzz of edgy gnats
that won't be brushed away –

Payment first, says the dealer in coal
no goods for an empty purse.

Not now, not now
cries the Knight of the Bucket
who would lengthen a story to stretch out time
postpone it and save it or waste it and whisper
what if, what if, what if ...
Kafka shivers, coughs in Berlin,
is anxious to put this tale to bed,
his hands are frozen, his fingers stiff.

So a woman shakes her apron and our hero
wafts away –
how slight a breeze will make a stir
like leaf-fall on an autumn day
how slight a breeze.

The author lets his beggar go
over the hills and far away.
Nimmerwiedersehen, he writes.

Does this word mean
he is lost forever (so final a phrase)
or is he invisible, swathed in a cloak
that hides his human ragged form
and keeps him alive
beyond the hills of ice?

How light a quark of difference here
in this one word.

Kafka's ill, too tired to care.
He adds a stop and blots his pages
puts the fragment away.

REMEMBER WHEN WE TRIED

We tried to protect the growing grain
by killing off the sparrow, once,
in a landscape swarming with men and boys
all running, shooting, shouting, beating
the air with fists. So hard a chase and the birds
so tired they fell in scores from emptying skies
while locusts, free of claws and beaks, hovered
above the succulent crops then plummeted
down, more after more, like a biblical plague
foretelling death, like a blinding, shocking rain.

FINE DETAIL

A nestling will open its tiny beak
for any shape of silhouette that flickers
above its eye

No need for finer detail here
nor when a cobweb in a stubble field
disperses in unbright air

Once there was a St Martin's summer
November days of dark-green rain
an after-the-harvest ceasing of war
the soothing of body's ache

Now this is a season for children to die
though a drone overhead has a detail of bird
and it's time for the faceless men to scurry
along a nowhere road

It's a season of loss a father says
as he carries home a scrap of torso
could be anybody's torso
and buries it as his son

NERVES OF A LEAF

I am un-leaving
in the pushing wind

and you
my feckless, temporal stem

would let me
detach, un-
loose my green dependence.

Now I will be rich
with autumn
tooth and saw-like
in my gloss

for this day

is muscular, not
a brown-crackle moment for shedding:
see how an early sun
shines.

NOT THE ONLY SONG

Remember Josie on the quayside, Neruda's voluptuous,
frenzied woman who arrived with a rug,
a sack of rice and a whole set

of Paul Robeson records? A clutch of belongings
to stave off the void where loneliness is wild strawberries
creeping, black sun sinking, shadow

under shadow, plankton in deep mud. You are so scared of
losing him, your lover – you'd crater the earth as a reindeer in
search of nourishing moss.

Go over to the window and notice how ice
is thin on the pond, how it melts over low lying carp who,
surviving winter, are now in a mind for spring.

Listen to the songs you once loved – listen then let them all go.
Better by far to be a neutrino, a particle burst from exploding
stars, an astrophysical

smidgen in the light. Convinced? What else can I say? Un-
soured by those siblings of Thanatos, those rancid and tainted
dishes of gloom, you will be

jouissance itself – a tree flower not a ground-hugging bud, no
Josie clinging on. A multitude of crickets, wasps and gnats will
rejoice: small singers in petal

and grass who cry *Love is not the only song*. Open that window
to skylines of tunes. The words will be new and your own.

SIX O'CLOCK

It's six o'clock, the end
of a difficult day for her,
too quiet and drearily long.
A walk, she thinks, will help.

By the river she slips on a pebble,
stumbles, falls,
bruises a bone in her foot.

And at 6 o'clock
city fog, yellow as bile
thickens over a skyline
that's low, industrial, hot;
red as Whitechapel blood.

At this hour Vesuvius
erupts into fire.
Many who try to scream and run
are rigid in the lava flow
as is the family dog.

At twilight there's a stabbing
on the Roman Senate's steps.
I told you so, says a soothsayer,
dining out on the story for weeks.

At six o'clock
the first of fifty-six wooden posts
is placed in the soil of a Salisbury henge
as the last slave dies and a man begins
to fashion a wheel, puts notches
in a wooden pipe, scratches
his thoughts in clay ...

Another girl by a windy shore
gathering kelp to feed her man, touches the curve
of a small white stone and notices
the crimson sun although she has no way
of telling time
except through loss of light –

but there's new life inside her
that kicks and turns with the urge to be born
and so she journeys on

not dreaming her descendant –
a shy young man
will one day happen to see a girl
trip over a stone and hurry
to help her get to her feet, will tend
her bruises, make this hour
of six o'clock
much brighter for them both.

CHILDREN OF ODE

Hedgerows are full of birds, to each his twig.
The jongleur in the courtyard
whistles and hums at his lady's feet
plucks his lyre to the fountains' fall
casts his glamorous *ode* of love over a high

Italian wall and into the rain with a westerly wind
to where the bittern in the byre
bombleth his own bass note.

As does the miller on the Dee who cares
for nobody, no not he, for his drone is heavy
his burden dull.

This muse of song was the last to leave
the Golden Age.
Somewhere her nickelodeon
plays 'Music Music Music'.

'Now Here Come I' – Morris Men and Mummers
in a flounce of ribbons, feathers and bells, a furbelow
of antic buffoons, so good for a laugh
before our revels all must end –

It's *Comedy's* turn to skid once more
on the skin of a ripe banana
to fall, pick up, get a quick dust down
and start all over again.

Parody, you mock.
A mung bean of spite
green with envy
you are a photo-copied copy of a copy.

There is not an original bone in your frame –
only burlesque, pastiche
and lampoon.

And here is Keats' nightingale
his *Melody*
a mellow, welcome guest.

With her as guide
a cluster of lonely, unattached notes
becomes an entity.

She is the poet's plaintive anthem
a swan's long wing
light beneath a leaf.

Enter *Tragedy* robed in black.
Nothing, she says, can affect the end, nothing
shall come of nothing
with blood begetting blood...

But now dream back:
Imagine a blue Athenian sky
goats on a hillside, pipes of Pan
the harvesting of the grape.

Here wanders one who howls
Her name is *Threnody*, her role
to cast rue for pity and sprigs of rosemary
into the grave.

She sits by the coffin of Emerson's boy
'The darling who shall not return.'

Save the last waltz for the one you love –
keep this evening for *Rhapsody*

who, in blue
is songbird and minstrel
lyre and drone
a lyric of rain and the westerly wind
an ode to joy.

THE CHAIN OF BEING

Gold and dolphin, eagle and oak are sumptuous
on their pinnacles; oysters and barnacles have no hope
nor the bird that pecks for seed.

Lower than archangels the Virtues cling
to ladder rungs; flocks of them in white chiffon
singing with cherub and saint.

Pietas was the quiet one.
We glimpse her tending the household gods
at a time when a boy might offer up

the shavings of his stubble beard
and a girl on the eve of her wedding
would give them her dolls.

FOR LOVE OF A BURNING BUSH

You are desperate you say
    for a burning bush, ground
    that is quivering, winds

in a cave and a still
    small voice. So you'd be one
    of the prophets, under-

study a saint? You lust
    for manna from heaven:
    that flake-like substance sends

you out with the hoarfrost
    to look for white seeds
    like coriander's, or beads

of dew that dry before
    the sun. Fool, you are shrub
    not a vine that may grub,

hook, pierce, cling, climb. You are
    dust in barley, fossil
    in ancient, colossal

cliffs of bone. Now listen:
    you must resemble an orb-
    weaving spider whose cord

is a thin but tensile
    thread that drifts and arrives
    on a ladder's rung, high

as the saint you would be.
    There are no hosannas,
    no medals for manna's

uncovering. No one,
    as in the anecdote
    of the blind men who groped

an elephant to learn
    the truth of its frame,
    no one can tell the name

or essence of manna:
    for the child it is sweet
    pure honey, the youth feasts

on it like crusty bread,
    the elderly relish
    it as oil; unblemished.

PTOLEMY'S STARS

Tonight, in this countryside
the sky is a bright citadel
shining on dark water.

Ptolemy might still recognise
the 'serried multitude of stars'
whose fiery circling caused his heart

to leap and soar with joy.
How easy it is to imagine the creamy
Milky Way, heavy and thick

with luminous souls, the iridescent
dead of the day, who pause for an aeon
of feasting, before swimming on to a moon.

And easy to imagine that sad tale
of Adam and Eve whose first skin
shone like a halo in gold leaf

before their flesh
dried up with loss and dulled
to a mortal grey.

A departure of shine
for them and for us as we
stagger and doze, are wounded

in sleep, unaware
that as dreamers
we are becoming extinct.

Tonight there are many stars
in this firmament.
A salmon, essence of silver

glitters in its own dark sea.
How luminescent it is
and vulnerable.

Indigo Dreams Publishing Ltd
24, Forest Houses
Cookworthy Moor
Halwill
Beaworthy
Devon
EX21 5UU
www.indigodreams.co.uk